Gospel Extracts

from C. H. Spurgeon

GLH Publishing
Louisville, Kentucky

Originally published in 1899, by Passmore and Alabaster.
Public Domain

Footnotes have been added for clarity for some archaic terms.
© GLH Publishing, 2021

ISBN:
  Paperback 978-1-64863-103-0
  Epub 978-1-64863-072-9

CONTENTS

1. Active Employment
2. Affliction
3. Difficulty of Winning Attention
4. Backsliding
5. Bereavement
6. True Christianity
7. Christian Experience
8. Power of Communion with God
9. Strong Consolation
10. Dancing
11. Unbelief
12. Certainty of Death
13. Drunkenness Inexcusable
14. Experimental Evidence
15. A Looking-glass for Faults
16. Fear of God
17. The Work of Man
18. Frailty of Human Life
19. God with Us
20. Conceptions of God
21. Insensible Influence of the Gospel
22. Spreading the Gospel
23. Rejecting the Gospel
24. The Heart
25. Heaven
26. Hope
27. The Hypocrite Unmasked
28. Hypocrisy
29. Infidelity Short-lived
30. Infidel Books
31. The Cell of Ignorance
32. The Inspiration of the Bible
33. Jesus Only

34. Imitation of Jesus
35. Acquaintanceship with Christ
36. The All-sufficent Saviour
37. The Judgment
38. Love to Christ
39. Miracles
40. Necessity of the New Birth
41. The Triumphs of Peace
42. Prayer
43. Procrastination
44. Promises Countersigned by Faith
45. The Dignity of Christian Service
46. Courage Necessary
47. Do Something
48. Strength for Service
49. Personal Work
50. Unfaithful Service
51. The Song of Heaven and Earth
52. Salvation by Grace
53. Salvation by Works
54. Subtlety of Satan
55. Self-righteousness
56. The Common Prison
57. Bitten by a Serpent
58. The Sinner's Best Plea
59. Temptation
60. Free Thought

1. Active Employment

A little stream flowed through a manufacturing town. An unhappy little stream it was, for it was forced to turn huge wheels and heavy machinery, and it wound its miserable way through factories where it was dyed black and blue, until it became a foul and filthy ditch, and loathed itself. It felt the tyranny which polluted its very existence.

Now, there came a deliverer, who looked upon the streamlet, and said, "I will set thee free and give thee rest."

So he stopped up the water-course, and said, "Abide in thy place: thou shalt no more flow where thou art enslaved and defiled."

In a very few days the brooklet found that it had but exchanged one evil for another. Its waters were stagnating; they were gathering into a great pool, and desiring to find a channel. It was in its very nature to flow on, and it foamed and swelled, and pressed against the dam which stayed it. Every hour it grew more inwardly restless; it threatened to break the barrier, and it made all who saw its angry looks tremble for the mischief it would do ere long. It never found rest until it was permitted to pursue an active course along a channel which had been prepared for it among the meadows and corn fields. Then, when it watered the plains and made glad the villages, it was a happy streamlet, perfectly at rest.

So our souls are made for activity, and when we are set free from the activities of our self-righteousness and the slavery of our sin, we must do something, and we shall never rest until we find that something to do.

A Greek historian desired very intensely to say a word about the people of the city where he was born. He felt he could not write his history without saying something of his own native place, and accordingly he wrote this—"While Athens was building temples, and Sparta was waging war, my countrymen were doing nothing."

I am afraid there are too many Christians, of whom, if the book were written as to what they are doing in the church, it would have to be said, they have been doing nothing all their lives.

If we desire to glorify God we need not give up our business.

Some people get the notion into their heads that the only way in which they can live for God is by becoming ministers, missionaries or Bible women. Alas! how many of us would be shut out from any opportunity of magnifying the Most High if this were the case. The shepherds who went to Bethlehem and saw the infant Jesus in the manger, went back to the sheep-pens glorifying and praising God.

Beloved, it is not office, it is earnestness; it is not position, it is grace which will enable us to glorify God. God is most surely glorified in that cobbler's stall where the godly worker as he plies the awl sings of the Saviour's love. The name of Jesus is glorified by yonder carter as he drives his horse and blesses his God, or speaks to his fellow-labourer by the roadside, as much as by yonder divine who, throughout the country, like Boanerges, is thundering out the gospel. God is glorified by our abiding in our vocation.

Take care you do not fall out of the path of duty by leaving your calling, and take care you do not dishonour your profession while in it; think not much of yourselves, but do not think too little of your calling. There is no trade which is not sanctified by the gospel. If you turn to the Bible, you will find the most menial forms of labour have been in some way or other connected either with the most daring deeds of faith, or else with persons whose lives have been otherwise illustrious. Keep to your calling, brother, keep to your calling! Whatever God has made thee, when He calls thee abide in that, unless thou art quite sure that He calls thee to something else. The shepherds glorified God though they went to their trade.

The devotion of the cloisters is by no means equal to that of the man who is engaged in the battle of life; the devotion of the nunnery and the monastery is at best the heroism of a soldier who shuns the battle; but the devotion of a man in business life, who turns all to the glory of God, is the courage of one who seeks the thickest of the fray, and there bears aloft the grand old standard of Jehovah-nissi.

2. AFFLICTION

I have seen a little plant beneath an oak tree sheltered from the storm, and wind, and rain, and it felt pleased and happy to be so screened; but I have seen the woodman come with his axe and fell the oak, and the little plant has trembled with fear because its protection was removed.

"Alas! for me," it said, "the hot sun will scorch me, the driving rain will drown me, and the fierce wind will tear me up by the roots."

But instead of these dreadful results, the shelter being removed, the plant has breathed freer air, drunk more of the dews of heaven, received more of the light of the sun, and it has sprung up and borne flowers which else had never bloomed, and seeds that never else had sown themselves in the soil.

Be glad when God thus visits thee, when He takes away these overshadowing but dwarfing comforts, to make thee have a clear way between thee and heaven, so that heavenly gifts might come more plentifully to thee.

You must never judge by circumstances. Diamonds may be worried upon the wheel, and common pebbles may bathe at ease in the brook. The most wicked are permitted to clamber to the high places of the earth, while the most righteous pine at the rich man's gate, with dogs for their companions. Choice flowers full often grow amid tangled briars. Who has not heard of the lily among thorns? Where dwell the pearls? Do not the dark depths of the ocean conceal them, amid mire and wreck?

Judge not by appearances, for heirs of light may walk in darkness, and princes of the celestial line may sit upon dunghills. Men accepted of God may be brought very, very low, as Jonah was.

Blessed be God, the green pastures and the still waters, the shepherd's crook and pleasant company, are objects which are quite as familiar to the believer as the howling wilderness and the brandished rod!

Our afflictions are like weights, and have a tendency to bow us to the dust, but there is a way of arranging weights by means of wheels and pulleys, so that they will even lift us up. Grace, by its matchless art, has often turned the heaviest of our trials into occasions for heavenly joy. *"We glory in tribulations also."* We gather honey out of the rock, and oil out of the flinty rock.

There is an old story in the Greek annals of a soldier under Antigonus who had a disease about him, an extremely painful one, likely to bring him soon to the grave. Always first in the charge was this soldier, rushing into the hottest part of the fray, as the bravest of the brave. His pain prompted him to fight, that he might forget it; and he feared not death, because he knew that in any case he had not long to live.

Antigonus, who greatly admired the valour of his soldier, discovering his malady, had him cured by one of the most eminent physicians of the day; but alas! from that moment the warrior was absent from the front of the battle. He now sought his ease; for, as he remarked to his companions, he had something worth living for — health, home, family, and other comforts, and he would not risk his life now as afore-times.

So, when our troubles are many, we are often by grace made courageous in serving our God. We feel that we have nothing to live for in this world, and we are driven, by the hope of the world to come, to exhibit zeal, self-denial, and industry. But how often is it otherwise in better times, for then the joys and pleasures of this world make it hard for us to remember the world to come, and we sink into inglorious ease.

3. Difficulty of Winning Attention

I have read of a minister who was surprised to observe that for some Sundays a rustic, whom he had never seen there before, now regularly made his appearance in church, but in the most open way in the world settled himself to sleep as soon as he was seated, and snored so loud that one heard him even during the singing.

A boy, to whom he had often spoken, and who had an open, merry expression of face, was in the habit of placing himself not far from the snorer. The minister now requested him to sit more immediately behind him, and to touch him from time to time in order to keep him awake. At first the lad refused to do this, but the promise of a penny led him to comply. During the whole service he could see the contest carried on between the little fellow and his somnolent neighbour, and by a glance of his eye he sought to encourage the former to keep up the rousing process.

On the following Sunday the rustic came again, and so did the boy, whom the minister begged to continue his good offices as before, but he declined. When he held out the bribe of the penny, the boy told him that the peasant had already given him two pennies, on condition that he should not be disturbed.

Let us do what we will to enlist the attention of our hearers, we shall not find it an easy task. With our illustrations and anecdotes we may, as it were, be giving one penny to secure the ear, but the world, the flesh, and the devil, with their cares, pleasures, and distractions, will always be offering two pennies to our one. Yet by God's grace we shall win the day, and conquer not alone the ear but the heart.

4. Backsliding

Decays in grace and backsliding are usually very much like the fall of the autumn leaves. You are watching the trees, for even now they are beginning to indicate the coming fall. They evidently know that their verdant robes are to be stripped from them, for they are casting off their first loose vestments. How slowly the time of the brown leaf comes on! You notice here and there a tinge of the copper hue, and anon the gold leaf or the bronze is apparent. Week after week you observe that the general fall of the leaves is drawing nearer, but it is a matter that creeps slowly on. And so with backsliders. They are not put out of the visible church all at once; they do not become open offenders all at once. The heart by slow degrees turns aside from the living God, and then at last comes the outward sin and the outward shame.

God save us from falling by little and little! The devil's little strokes have felled many great oaks. Constant droppings of temptation have worn away many stones. God save us therefrom! Some cities have been carried by storm. Brave soldiers have made the irons of the scaling ladder bite on the top of the wall, and up they have swarmed in defiance of death, and carried the city by sudden force within a few hours. But many other cities have been taken by the slow process of the siege;

the supplies have been cut off; warriors have been slain at the sally-ports; slowly entrenchments have been thrown up nearer and nearer to the wall; mines have been dug under the bastions; forts have been weakened; gates have been shaken; and at last the city has been subdued. Where Satan captures one man by force of strong temptation, he captures ten by the gradual process of sapping and undermining the principles which should rule within.

It is regarded by many as a law of nature, that our first love for Christ must grow cold, and our early zeal must necessarily decline. I do not believe it for a moment. *"The path of the just is as the shining light, that shineth more and more unto the perfect day"*; and, were we watchful and careful to live near to God, there is no reason why our spiritual life should not continuously make progress both in strength and beauty.

5. BEREAVEMENT

We remember to have heard a preacher at a funeral most beautifully setting forth this parable: "A certain nobleman had a spacious garden, which he left to the care of a faithful servant, whose delight it was to train the creepers along the trellis, to water the seeds in the time of drought, to support the stalks of the tender plants, and to do every work which could render the garden a Paradise of flowers."

"One morning he rose with joy, expecting to tend his beloved flowers, and hoping to find his favourites increased in beauty. To his surprise, he found one of his choicest beauties rent from its stem, and, looking around him, he missed from every bed the pride of his garden, the most precious of his blooming flowers."

"Full of grief and anger, he hurried to his fellow-servants, and demanded who had thus robbed him of his treasures. They had not done it, and he did not charge them with it; but he found no solace for his grief till one of them remarked: 'My lord was walking in the garden this morning, and I saw him pluck the flowers and carry them away.'"

"Then truly he found he had no cause for his trouble. He felt it was well that his master had been pleased to take his own, and he went away, smiling at his loss, because his lord had taken them."

"So," said the preacher, turning to the mourners, "you have lost one whom you regarded with much tender affection. The bonds of endearment have not availed for her retention upon earth. I know your wounded feelings when, instead of the lovely form which was the embodiment of all that is excellent and amiable, you behold nothing but ashes and corruption. But remember, my beloved, the Lord hath done it. He hath removed the tender mother, the affectionate wife, the inestimable friend. I say again, remember your own Lord has done it; therefore do not murmur, or yield yourselves to an excess of grief."

There was much force as well as beauty in the simple allegory: it were well if all the Lord's family had grace to practice its heavenly lesson, in all times of bereavement and affliction.

6. True Christianity

There is free toleration in this country to everything—permit me to say—toleration to everything but Christ. You will discover that the persecuting spirit is now as much abroad as ever. There are still men at whom it is most fashionable to sneer. We never scoff at Christians nowadays; we do not sneer at that respectable title, lest we should lose our own honour; we do not nowadays talk against the followers of Jesus under that name. No; but we have found out a way of doing it more safely.

There is a pretty word of modern invention—a very pretty word—the word *"Sectarian"*. Do you know what it means? A sectarian means a true Christian; a man who can afford to keep a conscience, and does not mind suffering for it; a man who, whatever he finds to be in that old Book, believes it, and acts upon it, and is zealous for it.

I believe that the men aimed at under the term, "sectarians," are the true followers of Christ, and that the sneers and jeers and all the nonsense that you are always reading and hearing, are really aimed at the Christian, the true Christian, only he is disguised and nicknamed by the word "sectarian." I would give not a farthing for your religion unless you sometimes win that title. If God's Word be true, every atom of it, then we should act upon it; and whatsoever the Lord commandeth, we should diligently keep and obey, remembering that our Master tells us if we break one of the least of His commandments, and teach men so, we shall be least in His kingdom. We ought to be very jealous, very precise, very anxious, that even in the minutiae of our Saviour's laws, we may obey, having our eyes up to Him as the eyes of servants are to their mistresses. But if you do this, you will find you are not tolerated, and you will get the cold shoulder in society.

A zealous Christian will find as truly a cross to carry nowadays as in the days of Simon the Cyrenian. If you will hold your tongue, if you will leave sinners to perish, if you will never endeavour to propagate your faith, if you will silence all witnessing for truth, if, in fact, you will renounce all the attributes of a Christian, if you will cease to be what a Christian must be, then the world will say, "Ah! that is right; that is the religion we like." But if you will believe, believe firmly, and if you will let your belief actuate your life, and if your belief is so precious that you feel compelled to spread it, then at once you will find that there is no room for Christ even in public sentiment, where everything else is received. Be an infidel, and none will therefore treat you contemptuously; but be a true Christian, and many will despise you.

Perhaps you know the legend, or, perhaps, true history, of the awakening of St. Augustine.

He dreamed that he died, and went to the gates of heaven, and the keeper of the gates said to him, "Who are you?"

He answered, *"Christianus sum:* I am a Christian."

The porter replied, "No, you are not a Christian. You are a Ciceronian, for your thoughts and studies were most of all directed to the works of Cicero and the classics, and you neglected the teaching of Jesus. We judge men here by that which most engrossed their thoughts, and you are judged not to be a Christian but a Ciceronian."

When Augustine awoke, he put aside the classics which he had studied, and the eloquence at which he had aimed, and he said, "I will be a Christian, and a theologian"; and from that time he devoted his thoughts to the Word of God, and his pen and his tongue to the instruction of others in the truth.

Oh! I would not have it said of any of you, "Well, he may be somewhat Christian, but he is far more a keen money-getting tradesman." I would not have it said, "Well, he may be a believer in Christ, but he is a good deal more of a politician." "Perhaps he is a Christian, but he is most at home when he is talking about science, farming, engineering, horses, mining, navigation, or pleasure-taking." No, no! you will never know the fulness of the joy which Jesus brings to the soul, unless under the power of the Holy Spirit you take the Lord your Master to be your All-in-all, and make Him the fountain of your intensest.

7. Christian Experience

A discussion arose between some members of a Bible-class, in reference to *the first* Christian exercise of the converted soul.

One contended that it was *penitence* or *sorrow;* another that it was *fear,* another *love,* another *hope,* another *faith,* for how could one fear or repent without belief?

Elder G—, overhearing the discussion, relieved the minds of the disputants with this remark: "Can you tell which spoke of the wheel moves first? You may be looking at one spoke, and think that it moves first, but they all start together. Thus, when the Spirit of God operates upon the human heart, all the graces begin to affect the penitent soul, though the individual may be more conscious of one than another."

8. Power of Communion with God

In driving piles, a machine is used by which a huge weight is lifted up and then made to fall upon the head of the pile. Of course the higher the weight is lifted, the more powerful is the blow which it gives when it descends.

Now, if we would tell upon our age and come down upon society with ponderous blows, we must see to it that we are uplifted as near to God as possible. All our power will depend upon the elevation of our spirits. Prayer, meditation, devotion, communion, are like a windlass to wind us up aloft. It is not lost time which we spend in such sacred exercises, for we are thus accumulating force, so that when we come down to our actual labour for God, we shall descend with an energy unknown to those to whom communion is unknown.

9. Strong Consolation

What is strong consolation? I think strong consolation is that which does not depend upon bodily health.

What a cowardly old enemy the devil is! When we are strong and vigorous in body, it is very seldom that he will tempt us to doubt and fear; but if we have been racked with hours of pain and sleepless nights, and are getting to feel faint and weary, then he comes in with his horrible insinuations: "God will forsake you. His promise will fail!" He is vile enough to put his black paws on the brightest truth in the Bible, ay, upon even the very existence of God Himself, and turn the boldest believer into the most terrible doubter, so that we seem to have gone bodily over to the army of Satan and to be doubting every good thing that is in the Word of God. Strong consolation, even at such times, enables us still to rejoice in the Lord though every nerve should twinge, and every bone should seem melted into jelly with pain. *"Though He slay me, yet will I trust in Him."* Let Him crush me, but He shall get nothing out of me but the wine of resignation. I will not fly in His face, but still say, "Not as I will, but as Thou wilt!" O may you have such strong consolation, my dear brethren.

10. Dancing

When I hear of a dancing party, I feel an uneasy sensation about the throat, remembering that a far greater preacher had his head danced off in the days of our Lord. However pleasing the polkas of Herodias might be to Herod, they were death to John the Baptist.

The caperings and wantonings of the ballroom are death to the solemn influences of our ministry, and many an ill-ended life first received its bent for evil amid the flippancies of gay assemblies met to trip away the hours.

11. UNBELIEF

There are degrees of punishment, but the highest degree is given to the man who rejects Christ. You have noticed that passage in the Bible, I daresay, that the liar and the whoremonger and the drunkard shall have their portion—who do you suppose with?—*unbelievers;* as if hell was made first of all for unbelievers, as if the pit was digged not for whoremongers and swearers and drunkards, but for men who despise Christ, because that is the A 1 sin, the cardinal vice, and men are condemned for that. Other iniquities come following after them, but this one goes before them to judgment.

Imagine for a moment that time has passed, and that the day of judgment is come. We are all gathered together, both quick and dead. The trumpet-blast waxes exceeding loud and long. We are all attentive, expecting something marvellous. The exchange stands still in its business; the store is deserted by the tradesman; the crowded streets are filled. All men stand still; they feel that the last great business-day is come, and that now they must settle their accounts forever. A solemn stillness fills the air; no sound is heard. All, all is noiseless.

Presently a great white cloud with solemn state sails through the sky, and then—hark the twofold clamour of the startled earth! On that cloud there sits one like unto the Son of Man. Every eye looks, and at last there is heard a unanimous shout—"It is He! It is He!" and after that you hear on the one hand, shouts of "Hallelujah, Hallelujah, Hallelujah, Welcome, Welcome, Welcome, Son of God!" but mixed with that there is a deep bass, composed of the weeping and the wailing of the men who have persecuted Him, and who have rejected Him.

Listen! I think I can dissect the sonnet; I think I can hear the words as they come separately, each one of them rolling like a death knell. What say they? They say, "Rocks, hide us; mountains, fall upon us, hide us from the face of Him that sits upon the throne!" And shall you be among the number of those who say to the rocks, "Hide us"?

My impenitent reader, suppose for a moment that you have gone out of the world, and that you have died impenitent, and that you are among those who are weeping, and wailing, and gnashing their teeth. What will then be your terror! Blanched cheeks and knocking knees are nothing compared to thy horror of heart when thou shalt be drunken, but not with wine, and when thou shalt reel to and fro with the intoxication of amazement, and shall fall down and roll in the dust for horror and dismay. For there He comes, and there He is, with fierce, fire-darting eye; and now the time is come for the great division. The voice is heard, "Gather My people from the four winds of heaven, Mine elect, in whom My soul delighteth." They are gathered at the right hand, and there they are. And now saith He, "Gather up the tares, and bind them in bundles to burn." And you are gathered, and on the left hand there you are, gathered into the bundle. All that is wanted is the lighting of the pile. Where shall be the torch that shall kindle them? The tares are to be burned: where is the flame? The flame comes out of *His* mouth, and it is composed of words like these— *"Depart, ye cursed, into everlasting fire, in hell, prepared for the devil and his angels."*

Do you linger? *"Depart!"* Do you seek a blessing? *"Ye are cursed."* Do ye seek to escape? *It is everlasting fire.* Do ye stop and plead? *"I called and ye refused; I stretched out My hands, and ye regarded Me not; therefore I will mock at your calamity, I will laugh when your fear cometh."* "Depart, again, I say; depart forever!" And you are gone. And what is your reflection? Why, it is this: "Oh! would to God that I had never been born! Oh! that I had never heard the gospel preached, that I might never have had the sin of rejecting it." This will be the gnawing of the worm in your conscience—"I knew better, but I did not do better. As I sowed the wind, it is right I should reap the whirlwind. I was checked, but I would not be stopped. I was wooed, but I would not be invited. Now I see that I have murdered myself. Oh! thought above all thoughts most deadly. I am lost, lost, lost! And this is the horror of horrors—I have caused myself to be lost; I have put from me the gospel of Christ; my unbelief has destroyed me!"

12. Certainty of Death

"All flesh is grass."

The whole history of man may be seen in the meadow. He springs up green and tender, subject to the frosts of infancy which imperil his young life; he grows, he comes to maturity, he puts on beauty even as the grass is adorned with flowers, and the meads are bedecked with varied hues; but after awhile his strength departs, and his beauty is wrinkled, even as the grass withers, and is followed by a fresh generation, which withers in its turn. Like ourselves, the grass ripens but to decay. The sons of men come to maturity in due time, and then decline and wither as the green herb. Some of the grass is not left to come to ripeness at all, but the mower's scythe suddenly removes it, even as swift-footed death overtakes the careless children of Adam.

Right on the edge of our graves sometimes we are, and yet we sport and laugh as though we had a lease of life! You forget death, most of you. The cemetery is far out of town, but still you should not quite forget it, for the hearse goes to and fro with awful regularity, and the church-bell that tolls is not rusty, and those words, "Earth to earth, dust to dust, ashes to ashes," are still familiar to the ears of some of us. It will soon be your turn to die. You, too, must gather up your feet in the bed, and meet your father's God. God grant that you may then be found right with Him!

Little do I know upon whom these sentences may have a special bearing; but they may have a bearing, dear friend, upon you. Some of you are dressed in black. You have had to go to the grave mourning because of others. That black will soon be worn by others for you, and the place that now knows you shall know you no more forever. Oh! by the frailty of life, by the near approach of the Master, or by the certainty of death, I pray you see to it that you breathe the prayer, "Lord, give me of Thy grace." The Lord help you to pray it!

Death will be to many the season of greatest joy. They will climb to Pisgah's top with weary footsteps; but when once there, the vision of the landscape will make amends for all the toil. The brooks, and hills, and vales, with milk and honey flow: and their delighted eyes shall gaze upon their portion, their eternal heritage.

But, oh! how different will be their lot, if instead of this, "Tekel" shall be written upon them at the last, because they are found wanting. "O my God! my God! hast thou forsaken me? Am I, after all, mistaken? Have I played the hypocrite, and must I take the mask off now? Have I covered over the cancer? Have I worn a golden cloth over my leprous forehead, and must it be rent away? And must I stand the mock of devils and the laughter of all worlds? What! have I drunk of Thy cup, have I eaten with Thee in the streets, and must I hear Thee say, 'I never knew thee; depart from me, thou worker of iniquity?' Oh! must it be?" Then how hard will be the bed on which I die! How stuffed with thorns that pillow! How tortured and anguished my poor broken heart, when every prop is knocked away, and the house comes tumbling down about our ears; when every drop of comfort is dried up, and even here the thirsty spirit lacks a drop of cordial to afford it comfort!

13. Drunkenness Inexcusable

We sometimes talk of a man being "as drunk as a beast," but whoever heard of a beast being drunk? Why, it is more beastly than anything a beast ever does.

I do not believe that the devil himself is ever guilty of anything like that. I never heard even him charged with being drunk.

It is a sin which has no sort of excuse. Those who fall into it generally fall into other deadly vices. It is the devil's back-door to hell, and everything that is hellish; for he that once gives away his brains to drink, is ready to be caught by Satan for anything.

Oh! but while the drunkard cannot have eternal life abiding in him while he is such, is it not a joy to think of the many drunkards who have been washed and saved? This night there are sitting here, those who have done with their cups, who have left behind them their strong drink, and who have renounced the haunts of their debauchery. They are washed and cleansed, and when they think of the contrast between where they used to be on Sunday night and where they now are, they give echo to the question, "Is not this a brand plucked out of the fire?"

14. Experimental Evidence

I have been informed that not long ago a certain infidel lecturer gave an opportunity to persons to reply to him after his oration. Of course he expected that one or two rashly-zealous young men would rise to advance the common arguments for Christianity, which he was quite prepared, by hook or crook, to battle with or laugh down. Instead of reasoners, an old lady, carrying a basket, wearing an ancient bonnet, and altogether dressed in an antique fashion, which marked both her age and her poverty, came upon the platform.

Putting down her basket and umbrella, she began: "I paid threepence to hear of something better than Jesus Christ, and I have not heard it. Now, let me tell you what religion has done for me, and then tell me something better, or else you've cheated me out of the threepence which I paid to come in. Now," she said, "I have been a widow thirty years, and I was left with ten children, and I trusted in the Lord Jesus Christ in the depths of poverty, and He appeared for me and comforted me, and helped me to bring up my children so that they have grown up and turned out respectable. None of you can tell what the troubles of a poor lone woman are, but the Lord has made His grace all-sufficient. I was often very sore pressed, but my prayers were heard by my Father in heaven, and I was always delivered. Now, you are going to tell me something better than that—better for a poor woman like me! I have been to the Lord sometimes when I've been very low indeed, and there's been scarcely anything for us to eat, and I've always found His providence has been good and kind to me. And when I lay very sick, I thought I was dying, and my heart was ready to break at leaving my poor fatherless boys and girls, and there was nothing kept me up but the thought of Jesus and His faithful love to my poor soul; and you tell me that it was all nonsense. Those who are young and foolish may believe you, but after what I have gone through, I know there is a reality in religion and it is no fancy. Tell me something better than what God has done for me, or else, I tell you, you have cheated me out of my threepence. Tell me something better."

The lecturer was a good hand at an argument, but such a mode of controversy was novel, and therefore he gave up the contest, and merely said, "Really, the dear old woman was so happy in her delusion he should not like to undeceive her."

"No," she said, "that won't do. Truth is truth, and your laughing can't alter it. Jesus Christ has been all this to me, and I could not sit down in the hall and hear you talk against Him without speaking up for Him, and asking you whether you could tell me something better than what He has done for me. I've tried and proved Him, and that's more than you have."

Herein is power, logic invincible, reasoning not to be gainsayed. The testing, and proving of God, getting His love really shed abroad in the heart—this is the great internal evidence of the gospel.

15. A Looking-glass for Faults

You can see great faults in others, but, my dear brother, be sure to look in the looking-glass every morning, and you will see quite as many faults, or else your eyes are weak. If that looking-glass were to show you your own heart you would never dare look again. I fear you would even break the glass.

Old John Berridge, as old as he was good, had a number of pictures of different ministers round his room, and he had a looking-glass in a frame to match. He would often take a friend into the room and say, "That is Calvin, that is John Bunyan," and when he took him up to the looking-glass he would add, "and that is the devil."

"Why," the friend would say, "it is myself!" "Ah," said he, "there is the devil in us all." Being so imperfect, we ought not to condemn.

16. Fear of God

There is a kind of fear towards God from which we must not wish to be free. There is that awful, necessary, admirable, excellent fear which is always due from the creature to the Creator, from the subject to the king, ay, and from the child toward the parent. That holy, filial fear of God, which makes us dread sin and constrains us to be obedient to His command, is to be cultivated. *"We had fathers of our flesh, and we gave them reverence, shall we not be in subjection to the Father of spirits and live?"*

There is the *"fear of the Lord which is the beginning of wisdom."*

To have a holy awe of our most holy, just, righteous, and tender Parent is a privilege, not a bondage. Godly fear is not the "fear which hath torment"; perfect love doth not cast it out, but dwells with it in joyful harmony. The angels perfectly love God, and yet with holy fear they veil their faces as they approach Him; and when we shall in glory behold the face of God, and shall be filled with all His fulness, we shall not cease humbly and reverently to adore His Infinite Majesty. Holy fear is a work of the Holy Ghost, and woe unto the man who does not possess it! Let him boast as he may, his "feeding himself without fear" is a mark of his hypocrisy.

The fear which is to be avoided is *slavish fear;* the fear which perfect love casts out; that trembling which keeps us at a distance from God, which makes us think of Him as a Spirit with whom we can have no communion; as a Being who has no care for us except to punish us, and for whom consequently we have no care except to escape if possible from His terrible presence.

This fear sometimes arises in men's hearts from their thoughts dwelling exclusively upon the divine greatness. Is it possible to peer long into the vast abyss of Infinity and not to fear? Can the mind yield itself up to the thought of the Eternal, Self-existent, Infinite One without being filled, first with awe and then with dread? What am I? An aphis creeping upon a rosebud is a more considerable creature in relation to the universe of beings than I can be in comparison with God. What am I? A grain of dust, that does not turn the scale of the most delicate balance, is a greater thing to man than a man is to Jehovah. At best we are less than nothing and vanity. But there is more to abase us than this. We have had the impertinence to be disobedient to the will of this great One, and now the goodness and greatness of His nature are as a current against which sinful humanity struggles in vain, for the irresistible torrent must run its course and overwhelm every opponent. What does the great God seem to us out of Christ but a stupendous rock, threatening to crush us, or a fathomless sea, hastening to swallow us up? The contemplation of the divine greatness may of itself fill man with horror, and cast him into unutterable misery!

Each one of the sterner attributes of God will cause the like fear. Think of His *power*, by which He rolls the stars along, and lay thine hand upon thy mouth. Think of His *wisdom*, by which He numbers the clouds and settles the ordinances of heaven. Meditate upon any one of these attributes, but especially upon His *justice*, and upon that devouring fire which burns unceasingly against sin, and it is no wonder if the soul becomes full of fear. Meanwhile let a sense of sin with its great whip of wire flagellate the conscience, and man will dread the bare idea of God: for this is the burden of the voice of conscience to guilty man, "If thou wert an obedient creature, this God were still terrible to thee. What art thou that thou shouldst have any claims upon Him, for thou hast offended, thou hast lifted the hand of rebellion against the infinite majesty of Omnipotence—what can become of thee?"

17. THE WORK OF MAN

Men have said of many of their works, "They shall endure forever," but how much have they been disappointed! In the age succeeding the flood, they made the brick, they gathered the slime, and when they had piled old Babel's tower, they said, "This shall last forever." But God confounded their language; they finished it not. By His lightnings He destroyed it, and left it a monument of their folly. Old Pharaoh and the Egyptian monarchs heaped up their pyramids, and they said, "They shall stand forever," and so, indeed, they do stand; but the time is approaching when age shall devour even these.

So with all the proudest works of man, whether they have been his temples or his monarchies; he has written "Everlasting" on them, but God has ordained their end, and they have passed away. The most stable things have been evanescent as shadows and the bubbles of an hour, speedily destroyed at God's bidding. Where is Nineveh, and where is Babylon? Where the cities of Persia? Where are the high places of Edom? Where are Moab, and the princes of Ammon? Where are the temples of the heroes of Greece? Where the millions that have passed from the gates of Thebes? Where are the hosts of Xerxes, or where the vast armies of the Roman emperors? Have they not passed away? And though in their pride they said, "This monarchy is an everlasting one; this queen of the seven hills shall be called the eternal city," its pride is dimmed; and she who sat alone, and said, "I shall be no widow, but a queen forever," she hath fallen, hath fallen, and in a little while she shall sink like a millstone in the flood, her name being a curse and a byword, and her site the habitation of dragons and of owls. Man calls his works eternal—God calls them fleeting; man conceives that they are built of rock—God says, "Nay, sand, or worse than that—they are air." Man say he erects them for eternity—God blows but for a moment, and where are they? Like baseless fabrics of a vision, they are passed and gone forever.

18. Frailty of Human Life

You stand over the mouth of hell upon a single plank, and that plank is rotten. You hang over the jaws of perdition by a solitary rope, and the strands of that rope are snapping one by one. Frailer than the spider's web is your life, and yet that is the only thing which divides you from a world of despair. The slightest insect commissioned by God's providence may end your unhappy life. You know not where, or when, or how disease may overtake you. Death often floats in the atmosphere of the house of God. He may be looking through those stony eyeholes. The skeleton monarch may be looking at and marking you as his prey. Could Xerxes stand here tonight, could he have a little Christianity mingled with his philosophy, then doubtless the tears he wept as he saw his army, and remembered that in fifty years all would be dead, were nothing to those he would weep as he remembered that thousands this day found within the walls of churches and chapels, and tens of thousands who are not found in any sanctuary, within less time than that will be not only dead but damned!

19. GOD WITH US

I give you for a watchword "Emmanuel, God with us." You, the saints redeemed by blood, have a right to all this in its fullest sense; drink into it and be filled with courage.

Do not say, "We can do nothing." Who are ye that can do nothing? God is with you. Do not say "The church is feeble and fallen upon evil times"—nay, "God is with us."

We need the courage of those ancient soldiers who were wont to regard difficulties only as whetstones upon which to sharpen their swords. I like Alexander's talk, when they said there were so many thousands, so many millions, perhaps, of Persians.

"Very well," says he, "it is good reaping where the corn is thick. One butcher is not afraid of a thousand sheep."

I like even the talk of the old Gascon, who said when they asked him, "Can you and your troops get into that fortress? It is impregnable."

"Can the sun enter it?" said he.

"Yes."

"Well, where the sun can go we can enter."

Whatever is possible or whatever is impossible, Christians can do at God's command, for God is with us. Do you not see that the word, "God with us," puts impossibility out of all existence?

Hearts that never could else be broken Will be broken if God be with us. Errors which never else could be confuted can be overthrown by "God with us." Things impossible with men are possible with God. John Wesley died with that upon his tongue, and let us live with it upon our hearts: "The best of all is God with us."

During an earthquake that occurred a few years since, the inhabitants of a small village were much alarmed. One old lady whom they all knew showed great calmness and apparent joy.

At length one of the villagers addressed the old lady, and said, "Mother, are you not afraid?"

"No," she replied. "I rejoice to know that I have a God who can shake the world."

20. Conceptions of God

One day the Jungo-kritu, head pundit of the College of Fort William, who is truly learned in his own shastras, gave from one of their books this parable on the subject of God:—

"In a certain country there existed a village of blind men. These men had heard that there was an amazing animal called the elephant, but they knew not how to form an idea of his shape. One day an elephant happened to pass through the place, and the villagers crowded to the spot where the animal was standing. One of them got hold of his trunk, another seized his ear, another his tail, another one of his legs, etc."

"After thus trying to gratify their curiosity they returned into the village, and sitting down together they began to give their ideas on what the elephant was like. The man who had seized his trunk said he thought the elephant was like the body of the plantain tree. The man who had felt his ear said he thought he was like the fan with which the Hindoos clean the rice. The man who had felt his tail said he thought he must be like a snake, and the man who had seized his leg thought he must be like a pillar."

"An old blind man of some judgment was present, who was greatly perplexed how to reconcile these jarring notions, respecting the form of the elephant; but he at length said: 'You have all been to examine this animal, it is true; and what you report cannot be false, I suppose; therefore, that which was like the plantain tree must be his trunk; that which was like a fan must be his ear; that which was like a snake must be his tail, and that which was like a pillar must be his body.' In this way the old man united all their notions, and made out something of the form of the elephant."

"Respecting God," added the pundit, "we are all blind. None of us has seen Him. Those who wrote the shastras, like the old blind man, have collected all the reasonings and conjectures of mankind together, and have endeavoured to form some idea of the nature of the Divine Being."

The pundit's parable may be appropriately applied to the science of theology. Some Christians see one truth and some another, and each one is quite sure that he has beheld the whole. Where is the master mind who shall gather up the truth out of each creed, and see the theology of the Bible in its completeness?

21. Insensible Influence of the Gospel

There is a lavender field over yonder, and though a man may hate the smell of it, and block up his windows and keep his doors closed, somehow or other, he may depend upon it, when the wind blows in the right direction, the perfume will reach him. And so it is here; if a man will not listen to the preaching of the gospel, if he constantly neglects attendance upon the means of grace, yet for all that, the kingdom of heaven has come nigh to him, and in some form or other the angel of mercy will frequently cross his path.

22. Spreading the Gospel

Huber, the great naturalist, tells us that if a single wasp discovers a deposit of honey or other food, he will return to his nest and impart the good news to his companions, who will sally forth in great numbers to partake of the fare which has been discovered for them.

Shall we who have found honey in the rock Christ Jesus be less considerate of our fellow-men than wasps are of their fellow-insects? Ought we not rather, like the Samaritan woman, hasten to tell the good news? Common humanity should prevent one of us from concealing the great discovery which grace has enabled us to make.

23. Rejecting the Gospel

Bring me here a Hottentot, or a man from Kamschatka, a wild savage who has never listened to the Word. That man may have been guilty of every sin in the catalogue of guilt except one; but that one I am sure he has not committed. He has not committed the sin of rejecting the gospel when it was preached to him. But you, when you hear the gospel, have an opportunity of committing a fresh sin; and if you have rejected it, you have added a fresh iniquity to all those others that hang about your neck.

24. The Heart

Inasmuch as the heart is the most important part of man—for out of it are the issues of life—it would be natural to expect that Satan, when he intended to do mischief to mankind, would be sure to make his strongest and most perpetual attacks upon the heart.

What we might have guessed in wisdom is certainly true in experience; for though Satan will tempt and try us in every way, though every gate of the town of Mansoul may be battered, though against every part of the walls thereof he will be sure to bring out his great guns, yet the place against which he levels his deadliest malice and his most furious strength, is the heart. Into the heart, already of itself evil enough, he thrusts the seeds of every evil thing, and doth his utmost to make it a den of unclean birds, a garden of poisonous trees, a river flowing with destructive water.

Hence arises the necessity that we should be doubly cautious in keeping the heart with all diligence; for if, on the one hand, it be the most important, and, on the other hand, Satan, knowing this, makes his most furious and determined attacks against it, then, with double force the exhortation comes, *"Keep thy heart with all diligence."* And the promise also becomes doubly sweet from the very fact of the double danger—the promise which says: *"The peace of God shall keep your hearts and minds through Christ Jesus our Lord."*

25. HEAVEN

Such a thing as a funeral knell was never heard in heaven. No angel was ever carried to his grave—though angels have been in the sepulchre, for there sat two, at the head and the feet, where the body of Jesus had lain; but they were visitors, not dwellers there. There is nothing about angels upon which the death-worm can feed; no sepulchre could encase their free spirits, and the bonds of death could not hold them for a moment. So is it with the freed ones who have passed through the grave and are now with Christ—they cannot die. Ages upon ages may roll on, eternity's ceaseless cycles may continue, but there shall be no grey hairs of decay upon the heads of the immortals. Celestials shall never decay.

Let me imagine a man entering heaven without a change of heart. He comes within the gates. He hears a sonnet. He starts! It is to the praise of his *enemy*. He sees a throne, and on it sits one who is glorious; but it is his *enemy*. He walks streets of gold, but those streets belong to his *enemy*. He sees hosts of angels, but those hosts are the servants of his *enemy*. He is in an *enemy's* house; for he is *at enmity* with God. He could not join the song, for he would not know the tune. There he would stand, silent, motionless, till Christ would say, with a voice louder than ten thousand thunders, "What dost thou here? Enemies at a marriage banquet? Enemies in the children's house? Enemies in heaven? Get thee gone! 'Depart, ye cursed into everlasting fire in hell!'"

Heavenly joys shall be like the tree of life in the New Jerusalem, which brings forth twelve manner of fruits, and yields her fruit every month.

Robert Hall used to cry: "O, for the everlasting rest!" but Wilberforce would sigh to dwell in unbroken love. Hall was a man who suffered—he longed for rest; Wilberforce was a man of amiable spirit, loving society and fellowship—he looked for love. Hall shall have his rest, and Wilberforce shall have his love. There are joys at God's right hand, suitable for the spiritual tastes of all those who shall come thither. The heavenly manna tastes to every man's peculiar liking.

"Who," saith an old divine, "chides a servant for taking away the first course at a feast when the second consists of far greater delicacies?" Who then can feel regret that this present world passeth away, when he sees that an eternal world of joy is coming? The first course is grace, but the second is glory, and that is as much better as the fruit is better than the blossom.

26. HOPE

Once on a time certain labourers were sent forth by a great king to level a primeval forest, to plow it, sow it, and bring him the harvest.

They were stout-hearted and strong, and willing enough for labour, and much they needed all their strength and more. One stalwart labourer was named Industry—consecrated work was his. His brother Patience, with thews of steel, went with him, and tired not in the longest days under the heaviest labours. To help them they had Zeal, clothed with ardent and indomitable energy. Side by side there stood his kinsman Self-denial, and his friend Importunity. These went forth to their labour, and they took with them, to cheer their toils, their well-beloved sister Hope; and well it was they did, for they needed the music of her consolation ere the work was done, for the forest trees were huge, and demanded many sturdy blows of the axe ere they would fall prone upon the ground.

One by one the giant forest-kings were overthrown, but the labour was immense and incessant. At night when they went to their rest, the day's work always seemed so light, for as they crossed the threshold, Patience, wiping the sweat from his brow, would be encouraged, and Self-denial would be strengthened, by hearing the sweet voice of Hope within singing, "God will bless us, God, even our own God, will bless us." They felled the lofty trees to the music of that strain; they cleared the acres one by one, they tore from their sockets the huge roots, they delved the soil, they sowed the corn, and waited for the harvest, often much discouraged, but still held to their work as by silver chains and golden fetters by the sweet sound of the voice which chanted so constantly, "God, even our own God, will bless us." They never could refrain from service, for Hope never could refrain from song. They were ashamed to be discouraged, they were shocked to be despairing, for still the voice ran clearly out at noon and eventide, "God will bless us, God, even our own God, will bless us."

You know the parable, you recognize the voice: may you hear it in your souls!

It is reported that in the Tamil language there is no word for *hope*. Alas! poor men, if we were all as destitute of blessed comfort itself as these Tamil speakers are of the word! What must be the misery of souls in hell where they remember the word, but can never know hope itself!

27. THE HYPOCRITE UNMASKED

O hypocrite, thou thinkest that thou shalt excel because the minister has been duped and gives thee credit for a deep experience; because the deacons have been entrapped and think thee to be eminently godly; because the church members receive thee to their houses, and think thee a dear child of God, too! Poor soul! mayhap thou mayest go to thy grave with the delusion in thy brain that all is right with thee; but remember, though like a sheep thou art laid in thy grave, death will find thee out. He will say to thee: "Off with thy mask, man! away with all thy robes! Up with that whitewashed sepulchre! Take off that green turf; let the worms be seen. Out with the body; let us see the reeking corruption!"

What wilt thou say when thine abominably corrupt and filthy heart shall be opened before the sun, and when men and angels shall hear thy lies and hypocrisies laid bare before them? Wilt thou play the hypocrite then? Soul, come and sing God's praises in the day of judgment with false lip! Tell Him now, while a widow's house is in your throat, tell Him that you love Him! Come, now, thou that devourest the fatherless, thou that robbest, thou that dost uncleanness; tell Him now that thou didst make thy boast in the Lord; tell Him that thou didst preach His word; tell Him that thou didst walk in His streets; tell Him thou didst make it known that thou wert one of the excellent of the earth!

What, man! is thy babbling tongue silent for once? What is the matter with thee? Thou wast never slow to talk of thy godliness. Speak out, and say: "I took the sacramental cup; I was a professor."

Oh, how changed! The whitewashed sepulchre has become white in another sense; he is white with horror. See now! the talkative has become dumb; the boaster is silent; the formalist's garb is rent to rags, the moth has devoured their beauty. Their gold has become tarnished, and their silver cankered. Ah! it must be so with every man who has thus belied God and his own conscience.

28. Hypocrisy

In the pursuit of pastoral duty, I stood a little while ago in a cheesemonger's shop, and being in a fidgety humour, and having a stick in my hand, I did what most Englishmen are sure to do—I was not content with seeing, but must needs touch as well. My stick came gently upon a fine cheese in the window, and to my surprise a most metallic sound emanated from it. The sound was rather hollow, or one might have surmised that all the taste holes had been filled up with sovereigns, and thus the cheese had been greatly enriched, and the merchant had been his own banker. There was, however, a sort of crockery jingle in the sound, like the ring of a huge bread or milk pan, such as our country friends use so abundantly, and I came to the very correct conclusion that I had found a very well-got-up hypocrite in the shop window.

From that time, when I pass by, I mentally whisper, "Pottery"; and the shams may even be exchanged for realities, but I shall be long in believing it. In my mind the large stock has dissolved into potsherds, and the fine show in the window only suggests the potter's vessel.

The homely illustration is simply introduced because we find people of this sort in our churches, looking extremely like what they should be, yet having no substance in them, so that if accidentally one happens to tap them somewhere or other with sudden temptation or stern duty, the baked earth gives forth its own ring, and the pretender is esteemed no longer.

29. Infidelity Short-lived

Every age produces a new crop of heretics and infidels. Just as the current of the times may run, so doth the stream of infidelity change its direction.

We have, lived long enough, some of us, to see three or four species of atheists and deists rise and die, for they are short-lived, an ephemeral generation. We have seen the church attacked by weapons borrowed from geology, ethnology and anatomy, and then from the schools of criticism fierce warriors have issued; but she survives all her antagonists. She has been assailed from almost every quarter, but the fears that tarry in the church today are blown to the wind tomorrow; yea, the church has been enriched by the attacks, for her divines have set to work to study the points that were dubious, to strengthen the walls that seemed a little weak, and so her towers have been strengthened, and her bulwarks consolidated.

30. Infidel Books

I am asked sometimes to read an heretical or an infidel book. Well, if I believed my reading it would help its refutation, and might be an assistance to others in keeping them out of error, I might do it as a hard matter of duty; but I shall not do it unless I see some good will come from it. I am not going to drag my spirit through a ditch for the sake of having it washed afterwards, for it is not my own. It may be that good medicine would restore me if I poisoned myself with putrid meat, but I am not going to try it. I dare not experiment on a mind which no longer belongs to me.

There is a mother and a child, and the child has a book to play with, and a black-lead pencil. It is making drawings and marks upon the book, and the mother takes no notice. It lays down one book and snatches another from the table, and at once the mother rises from her seat, and hurriedly takes the book away, saying: "No, my dear, you must not mark that, for it is not ours."

So with my mind, intellect and spirit; if it belonged to me I might or might not play tomfool with it, and go to hear infidels and such-like preach, but as it is not my own I will preserve it from such fooleries, and the pure Word shall not be mingled with the errors of men.

31. THE CELL OF IGNORANCE

Methought I once entered the cell of ignorance. I groped as a blind man gropeth for the wall. I was guided by my ear by sobs and moans to a spot where there knelt a creature in an earnest agony of prayer. I asked him what made his cell so dark. I knew the door was made of *unbelief*, which surely shuts out all light, but I marvelled why this place should be so dark, only I recollected to have read of some that sat *"in darkness, and in the shadow of death, being bound in affliction and iron."*

I asked him if there were no windows to the cell. Yes, there were windows, many windows, so people told him, but they had been stopped up years ago and he did not know the way to open them. He was fully convinced that they never could afford light *to him.*

I felt for one of the ancient lightholes, but it seemed as if, instead of giving light, it emitted darkness. I touched it with my hand, and it felt to me to have once been a window such as I had gazed through with delight. He told me it was one of the doctrines of grace which had greatly perplexed him; it was called *Election*. He said he should have had a little light had it not been for that doctrine, but since God had chosen His people, and he felt persuaded that He had not chosen him, he was lost forever since if he were not chosen, it was hopeless for him to seek for mercy.

I went up to that window and pulled out some handfuls of rags; filthy rotten rags, which some enemies of the doctrine had stuffed into the opening; caricatures and misrepresentations of the doctrine, maliciously used to injure the glorious truth of divine sovereignty. As I pulled out these rags, light streamed in, and the man smiled as I told him, "It is a mercy for thee that there is such a doctrine as election, for if there were no such doctrine there would be no hope for thee. Salvation must either be by God's will or by man's merit; if it were by man's merit, thou wouldst never be saved; but since it is by God's will, and He will have mercy on whom He will have mercy, there is no reason why He should not have mercy on thee, even though thou mayest be the chief of sinners. Meanwhile He bids thee believe in His Son Jesus, and gives thee His divine word for it, that *him that cometh unto Him He will in no wise cast out!*"

The little light thus shed upon the poor man led him to seek for more, so he pointed to another darkened window which was called — *The Fall, or Human Depravity*.

The man said: "Oh, there is no hope for me, for I am totally depraved, and my nature is exceeding vile; there is no hope for me."

I pulled the rags out of this window, too, and I said to him: "Do you not see that your ruin fits you for the remedy? It is because you are lost that Christ came to save you. Physicians are for the sick, robes for the naked, cleansing for the filthy, and forgiveness for the guilty."

He said but little, but he pointed to another window, which was one I had long looked through and seen my Master's glory by its means; it was the doctrine of *Particular Redemption*.

"Ah!" said he, "suppose Christ has not redeemed me with His precious blood? Suppose He has never bought me with His death?"

I knocked out some old bricks which had been put in by an unskilful hand, which yet blocked out the light, and I told him that Christ did not offer a mock redemption, but one which did really redeem, for *"the blood of Jesus Christ, God's Son, cleanseth us from all sin."*

"Ah!" he said, "but suppose I am not one of the 'us'?"

I told him that he that believeth and trusteth Christ is manifestly one of those whom Jesus came to save, for he is saved. I told him that inasmuch as universal redemption manifestly does not redeem all, it was unworthy of his confidence; but a ransom which did redeem all believers, who are the only persons for whom it was presented, was a sure ground to build upon.

There were other doctrines like these. I found the man did not understand one of them; that the truth had been misrepresented to him, that he had heard the doctrines of grace falsely stated and caricatured, or else had never heard them at all. He had been led by some blind guide who had led him into the ditch, and now when the windows were opened and the man could see, he saw written over the door, "Believe and live!" and in the new light which he had found he trusted his Lord and Saviour, and walked out free, and marvelled that he had been so long a slave. I marvelled not, but I thought in my heart how accursed are those teachers who hide the light from the eyes of men so that they understand not the way of life. Ignorant souls, who know not the plan of salvation, will have many sorrows which they might escape by instruction. Study your Bibles well, be diligent in attending upon a free-grace ministry, labour after a clear apprehension of the plan of salvation, and it will often please God that when you come to understand His truth your spirits will receive comfort, for it is by the truth that *"the Lord looseth the prisoners."*

32. THE INSPIRATION OF THE BIBLE

The inspiration of the Bible is verbal inspiration. In some cases it must have been only verbal; in every case it must have been mainly so. The human mind is not able to understand and to express all the thoughts of God, they are too sublime; and therefore God dictated to the prophets the very language which they should deliver—language of which they themselves could not see the far-reaching meaning. They did not themselves altogether understand what they were called to reveal, for the Holy Spirit often carried them beyond themselves, and made them utter more than they understood. They rejoiced in the testimony of the Spirit within them, but they were not free from the necessity to search, and to search diligently if they would for themselves derive benefit from the divine revelation. I know not how this is, but the fact is clearly stated and must be true. *"Of which salvation the prophets have enquired and searched diligently, who prophesied of the grace that should come unto you."*

Oh, my readers, how diligently you ought to search the Scriptures and listen to the saving word! If men that had the Holy Ghost, and were called "seers," nevertheless searched into the meaning of the word which they themselves spoke, what ought such poor things as we to do in order to understand the gospel? It should be our delight to read, mark, learn, and inwardly digest the doctrines of grace.

33. JESUS ONLY

"Jesus only."

Brethren, it is all the gospel we have to preach, it is all the gospel we want to preach. It is the only ground of confidence which we have for ourselves. It is all the hope we have to set before others. I know that in this age there is an overweening desire for that which has the aspect of being intellectual, deep and novel; and we are often informed that there are to be developments in religion even as in science; and we are despised as being hardly men, certainly not thinking men, if we preach today what was preached two hundred years ago. Brethren, we preach today what was preached eighteen hundred years ago, and wherein others make alterations they create deformities, and not improvements. We are not ashamed to avow that the old truth of Christ alone is everlasting. All else has gone or shall go, but the gospel towers above the wrecks of time. *"Jesus only"* remains as the sole topic of our ministry, and we want nothing else.

"Jesus only" shall be our reward. To be with Him where He is, to behold His glory, to be like Him when we shall see Him as He is, we ask no other heaven. No other bliss can our soul conceive of. The Lord grant we may have a fulness of this, and *"Jesus only"* shall be throughout eternity our delight.

I do desire for my fellow-Christians and for myself that more and more the great object of our thoughts, motives and acts may be *"Jesus only."* I believe that whenever our religion is most vital, it is most full of Christ. When it is most practical, downright and common sense, it always gets nearest to Jesus. I can bear witness that whenever I am in deeps of sorrow, nothing will do for me but *Jesus only*. I can rest in some degree in the externals of religion, its outward escarpments and bulwarks, when I am in health; but I retreat to the innermost citadel of our holy faith, namely, to the very heart of Christ, when my spirit is assailed by temptation, or besieged with sorrow and anguish. Whenever I have high spiritual enjoyments, enjoyments rich, rare, celestial, they are always connected with *Jesus only*. Other religious things may give some kind of joy, and joy that is healthy too, but the sublimest, the most inebriating, the most divine of all joys, must be found in *Jesus only*. In fine, I find if I want to labour much, I must live on *Jesus only*; if I desire to suffer patiently, I must feed on *Jesus only*; if I wish to wrestle with God successfully, I must plead *Jesus only*; if I aspire to conquer sin, I must use the blood of *Jesus only*; if I pant to learn the mysteries of heaven, I must search the teachings of *Jesus only*.

The Christian life is begun, continued, and perfected altogether in connection with the Lord Jesus Christ. This is a very great blessing.

Sometimes when you go a journey, you travel so far under the protection of a certain company, but then you have to change, and the rest of your journey may be performed under very different circumstances, upon quite another kind of line.

Now we have not so far to go to heaven in the guardian care of Jesus Christ, and then at a certain point to change, so as to have somebody else to be our leader, or some other method of salvation. No, He is the author and He is the finisher of our faith. If we begin aright, we begin with *"Christ is all"*; if we go on aright, we go on with *"Christ is all"*; and if we finish aright, we finish with *"Christ is all."*

It was a great delusion of some in Paul's day that after they had begun in the spirit, they hoped to be made perfect in the flesh; and there are some nowadays who begin as sinners resting upon Christ, but they want to go on as independent saints, resting on themselves. That will never do, brethren. It is not "Christ and Company," anyhow. The sinner knows that it must be Christ only, because he has nothing of his own; and the saint ought to know that it must be Christ only, because he has less than nothing apart from Christ. I believe that if we grow out of Christ, we grow in an unhealthy mushroom fashion. What we need is to grow up into Christ in all things, knowing Him more and more, and being more and more satisfied that He is what we need. This is really a healthy growth, and may God send more and more of it to us as long as ever we live! Blessed be His holy name, with us it is Christ in the morning, when we are young and full of strength; it is Christ at noon, when we are bearing the burden and heat of the day; and it is Christ at eventide, when we lean on the staff for very age, and the shadows lengthen, and the light is dim. Yea, and it shall be Christ only when the night settles down and death-shade curtains our last bed. In all circumstances and conditions we look to Jesus only. Are we in wealth? Christ crowns it. Are we in poverty? Christ cheers it. Are we in honour? Christ calms us. Are we in shame? Christ consoles us. Are we in health? He sanctifies it. Are we in sickness? He relieves it. As He is at all times the same in Himself, so He is the same to us. To the same Christ we must come and cling under every new circumstance. Our heart must abide faithful to her one only Lord.

Heaven itself, although it be a fertile land, flowing with milk and honey, can produce no fairer flower than the Rose of Sharon. Its highest joys mount no higher than the head of Jesus. Its sweetest bliss is found in His name alone. If we would know heaven, let us know Jesus; if we would be heavenly, let us love Jesus.

When you get to heaven, ye children of God, will ye praise any but your Master? Calvinists, today you love John Calvin; will you praise him there? Lutheran, today thou dost love the memory of that stern reformer; wilt thou sing the song of Luther in heaven? Follower of Wesley, thou hast a reverence for that evangelist; wilt thou in heaven have a note for John Wesley? None, none, none! Giving up all names and all honours of men, the strain shall rise in undivided and unjarring unison: *"Unto Him that loved us, that washed us front our sins in His blood, unto Him be glory forever and ever."*

34. Imitation of Jesus

Have you ever noticed how badly boys write at the bottom of the pages in their copy-books? There is the copy at the top, and in the first line they look at that; in the second line they copy their own imitation; in the third line they copy their imitation of their imitation, and so the writing grows worse and worse as it descends the page.

Now, the apostles followed Christ; the first fathers imitated the apostles; the next fathers copied the first fathers, and so the standard of holiness fell dreadfully; and now we are too apt to follow the very lees and dregs of Christianity, and we think if we are about as good as our poor, imperfect ministers or leaders in the church, that we shall do well and deserve praise. My brethren, cover up the mere copies and imitations, and live by the first line. Copy Jesus; *"He is altogether lovely"*; and if you can write by the first line, you will write by the truest and best model in the world.

35. Acquaintanceship with Christ

Witnesses about other things exaggerate, but witnesses concerning Jesus Christ always fall short. Painters have frequently won repute by making portraits fairer than the originals, but none can ever paint Jesus with a pencil that shall give too much of lustre to His noble face. He is so glorious that even angels who have seen Him all their lives, and bowed before Him where His splendour is best revealed, could not tell to man or to one another the thousandth part of His excellences. If you want to know Him, you must see Him for yourself. You must make Him your personal acquaintance. You must press by faith into the inner circle, and cry with the spouse, *"Let Him kiss me with the kisses of His mouth, for Thy love is better than wine."*

The Lord Jesus is no fair-weather friend, but one who loveth at all times—a brother born for adversity. This He proves to His beloved, not by mere words of promise, but by actual deeds of affection. As our sufferings abound, so He makes our consolations to abound.

36. THE ALL-SUFFICENT SAVIOUR

Oh! who shall measure the heights of the Saviour's all-sufficiency? First, tell how high is sin, and then remember that as Noah's flood prevailed over the tops of earth's mountains, so the flood of Christ's redemption prevails over the tops of the mountains of our sins. In heaven's courts there are today men that once were murderers, and thieves, and drunkards, and whoremongers, and blasphemers, and persecutors; but they have been washed—they have been sanctified. Ask them whence the brightness of their robes hath come, and where their purity hath been achieved, and they with united breath tell you that they have washed their robes, and made them white in the blood of the Lamb.

You know that in Solomon's temple there was no sound of hammer heard, for the stones were made ready in the quarries, and brought all shaped and marked so that the masons might know the exact spot in which they were to be placed; so that no sound of iron was needed. All the planks and timbers were carried to their right places, and all the catches with which they were to be linked together were prepared, so that there might not be even the driving of a nail. Everything was ready beforehand.

It is the same with us. When we get to heaven there will be no sanctifying us there, no squaring us with affliction, no hammering us with the rod, no making us meet there. We must be made meet here; and blessed be His name, Christ will do all that beforehand. When we get there, we shall not need angels to put this member of the church in one place, and that member in another; Christ who brought the stones from the quarry and made them ready, shall Himself place the people in their inheritance in paradise. For He has Himself said: *"If I go and prepare a place for you, I will come again and receive you unto Myself."* Christ shall be His own usher; He shall receive His people Himself; He shall stand at the gates of heaven Himself to take His own people, and to put them in their allotted heritage in the land of the blessed.

Jesus Christ excels Solomon, for He provides all the materials. He hews them Himself; He roughcasts them first, and then afterward, during life, polishes them till He makes them ready to transport them to the hill of God, whereon His temple is to be built.

I was thinking what a, pretty figure was that floating of the trees of Lebanon after being sawn into planks and made ready to be fixed as pillars of the temple—what a fine emblem of death! Is it not just so with us? Here we grow, and are at length cut down, and made ready to become pillars of the temple. Across the stream of death we are ferried by a loving hand, and brought to the port of Jerusalem, where we are safely landed, to go no more out forever, but to abide as eternal pillars in the temple of our Lord. Now, you know, the Tyrians floated these rafts; but no stranger, no foreigner, shall float us across the stream of death. It is remarkable that Jesus Christ always uses expressions with regard to His people which impute their death to Him alone. You will recollect the expression in the Revelation: *"Thrust in Thy sickle, and reap: for the time is come for Thee to reap; for the harvest of the earth is ripe."* But when He begins to reap, not the vintage (which represents the wicked that were to be crushed), but the harvest which represents the godly, then it is said: *"He that sat on the cloud thrust in His sickle."* He did not leave it to His angels, He did it Himself. It is so with the bringing of those planks, and the moving of those stones. I say no king of Tyre and Sidon shall do it: Jesus Christ Himself shall pilot us across the stream, and land us safe on Canaan's side.

37. THE JUDGMENT

Laugh at religion now! scoff at Christ now! now that the angels are gathering for the judgment, now that the trumpet sounds exceedingly loud and long, now that the heavens are red with fire, that the great furnace of hell o'erleaps its boundary, and is about to encircle thee in its flame. Now despise religion! Ah, no! I see thee. Now thy stiff knees are bending, now thy bold forehead, for the first time, is covered with hot sweat of trembling, now thine eyes that once were full of scorn are full of tears; thou dost look on Him whom thou didst despise, and thou art weeping for thy sin.

O sinner! it will be too late then. Where thou fallest, there thou liest. Where judgment finds thee, there eternity shall leave thee. Time shall be no more when judgment comes; and when time is no more, change is impossible! In eternity there can be no change, no deliverance, no signing of acquittal. Once lost, lost forever; once damned, damned to all eternity!

In hell there is no hope. They have not even the hope of dying—the hope of being annihilated. They are forever—forever—forever—lost! On every chain in hell there is written "forever." In the fires, there blazes out the words "forever." Up above their heads they read "forever." Their eyes are galled, and their hearts are pained with the thought that it is "forever." Oh! if I could tell you that hell would one day be burned out, and that those who were lost might be saved, there would be a jubilee in hell at the very thought of it. But it cannot be—they are *cast into outer darkness forever*.

Oh, bethink you that there is but one hope, and that one hope lost it is gone forever! Defeated in one battle, a commander attempts another, and hopes that he may yet win the campaign. Your life is your own fight, and if it is lost, it is lost forever. The man who was bankrupt yesterday commences in business again with good heart, and hopes that he may yet succeed; but in the business of this mortal life, if you are found bankrupt, you are bankrupt forever and ever.

I do therefore charge you, by the living God, before whom I stand and before whom I may have to give an account of this day's preaching ere another sun shall shine, I charge you to see to your own salvation.

38. LOVE TO CHRIST

Love to Christ smooths the path of duty, and wings the feet to travel it; it is the bow which impels the arrow of obedience; it is the mainspring moving the wheels of duty; it is the strong arm tugging the oar of diligence. Love is the marrow of the bones of fidelity, the blood in the veins of piety, the sinew of spiritual strength—yea, the life of sincere devotion. He that hath love can no more be motionless than the aspen in the gale, the sere leaf in the hurricane, or the spray in the tempest. As well may hearts cease to beat as love cease to labour. Love is instinct with activity, it cannot be idle. It is full of energy, it cannot content itself with littles. It is the well-spring of heroism, and great deeds are the gushings of its fountain. It is a giant—it heapeth mountains upon mountains, and thinks the pile but little. It is a mighty mystery, for it changes bitter into sweet. It calls death life, and life death, and it makes pain less painful than enjoyment.

Love has a clear eye, but it can see only one thing—it is blind to every interest but that of its Lord. It seeth things in the light of His glory, and weigheth actions in the scales of His honour. It counts royalty but drudgery if it cannot reign for Christ, but it delights in servitude as much as in honour if it can thereby advance the Master's kingdom. Its end sweetens all its means. Its object lightens its toil, and removes its weariness. Love, with refreshing influence, girds up the loins of the pilgrim, so that he forgets fatigue; it casts a shadow for the wayfaring man, so that he feels not the burning heat; and he puts the bottle to the lip of thirst.

"We love Him because He first loved us." Here is the starting-point of love's race. This is the rippling rill which afterward swells into a river—the torch with which the pile of piety is kindled. The emancipated spirit loves the Saviour for the freedom which He has conferred upon it. It beholds the agony with which the priceless gift was purchased, and it adores the bleeding sufferer for the pains which He so generously endured.

39. Miracles

Do you not know that we have miracles in the Christian Church still? Scoffers come to us and say, *"Work a miracle, and we will believe you."* We do work these miracles every day. Have you not heard persons assert that by the preaching of the gospel their lives have been completely changed? In the case of some the change is very obvious to all persons acquainted with them. How was this great change achieved? By the Holy Spirit, through the gospel of their salvation. I need not quote special cases. There are many who would tell you where they used to spend their Sabbaths, and what was their delight. All things have become new with them. They now seek after holiness as earnestly as they once pursued evil: though they are not what they want to be, they are not what they used to be. They never thought of purity or goodness, or anything of the kind, but they loved the wages of unrighteousness, and now they loathe the things they once loved.

I have seen moral miracles quite as marvellous in their line as the healing of a leper, or the raising of the dead. This is the witness of the Holy Ghost which He continues to bear in the church, and by that witness I entreat you to stop and think of the blessed salvation which can work the same miracle in you.

40. Necessity of the New Birth

I was staying one day at an inn in one of the valleys of Northern Italy, where the floor was dreadfully dirty. I had it in my mind to advise the landlady to scrub it, but when I perceived that it was made of mud, I reflected that the more she scrubbed the worse it would be.

The man who knows his own heart soon perceives that his corrupt nature admits of no improvement. There must be a new nature implanted, or the man will be only "washed to deeper stains." *"Ye must be born again."* Ours is not a case for mending, but for making new.

41. The Triumphs of Peace

Have you not noticed how magnificently Peace winneth its reprisals at the hands of War? Look through this country. Methinks if the angel of peace should go with us, as we journey through it, and stop at the various ancient towns where there are dismantled castles and high mounds from which every vestige of a building has long been swept, the angel would look us in the face, and say: "I have done all this. War scattered my peaceful subjects, burned down my cottages, ravaged my temples, and laid my mansions with the dust. But I have attacked War in his own strongholds and I have routed him. Walk through his halls. Can you hear now the tramp of the warrior? Where is now the sound of the clarion and the drum? The sheep is feeding from the cannon's mouth, and the bird builds his nest where once the warrior did hang his helmet."

As rare curiosities we dig up the swords and spears of our forefathers, and little do we reck[1] that in this we are doing tribute to Peace. For Peace is the conqueror. It hath been a long duel, and much blood hath been shed, but Peace hath been the victor. War, after all, has but spasmodic triumphs, and again it sinks—it dies; but Peace ever reigneth. If she be driven from one part of

---

1 That is "to pay heed to something."

the earth, yet she dwelleth in another; and while War, with busy hand, is piling up here a wall and there a rampart, and there a tower, Peace with her gentle finger is covering o'er the castle with moss and ivy, and casting stones from the top and levelling it with the ground.

42. Prayer

Two friends agree never to go farther apart than they can communicate with one another by telegraph. One of them has crossed the Atlantic, and resides in the United States, or in the far West, but still he has only to go to the office, where a wire can be touched and a message will flash to his friend in England, and tell him his needs.

This is just the compact God has made with His people. They shall never go where there is not a telegraphic communication between them and Himself. You may be out at sea, or in Australia, but the communication of prayer is always open between your soul and God, and if you were commanded to ride on the wings of the morning to the uttermost parts of the sea, or if for awhile you had to make your bed in the abyss, if you are His child, still will you be able to reach His heart.

I think it is Ambrose who uses a very pretty figure concerning believers' prayers. He says we are like little children who run into the garden to gather flowers to please their father, but we are so ignorant and childish that we pluck as many weeds as flowers, and some of them very noxious, and we would carry this strange mixture in our hands, thinking that such base weeds would be acceptable to him.

The mother meets the child at the door, and she says to it: "Little one, thou knowest not what thou hast gathered." She unbinds this mixture and takes from it all the weeds, and leaves only the sweet flowers, and then she takes other flowers sweeter than those which the child has plucked, and inserts them instead of the weeds, and then puts back the perfect posy into the child's hand, and it runs therewith to its father.

Jesus Christ in more than motherly tenderness thus deals with our supplications. If we could see one of our prayers after Christ Jesus has amended it, we should scarce know it again. He has such skill that even our good flowers grow fairer in His hand. We clumsily tied them into a bundle, but He arranges them into a fair bouquet, where each beauty enhances the charm of its neighbour. If I could see my prayer after the Lord has prayed it, I should miss so much, and I should find so much there that was none of mine, that I am sure its fullest acceptance with God would not cause me a moment's pride, but rather make me blush with grateful humility before Him whose boundless sweetness lent to me and my poor prayer a sweetness not our own. Though the prayers of God's people are as precious incense, they would never be a sweet smell unto God, were it not that they are *"accepted in the Beloved."*

Prayer is a certain forerunner of salvation. Sinner, thou canst not pray and perish; prayer and perishing are two things that never go together.

I ask you not what your prayer is; it may be a groan, it may be a tear, a wordless prayer, or a prayer in broken English, ungrammatical and harsh to the ear; but if it be a prayer from the inmost heart, thou shalt be saved; or else this promise is a lie: *"Whosoever shall call upon the name of the Lord shall be saved!"*

As surely as thou prayest, whoever thou mayest be, whatever thy past life, whatever the transgressions in which thou hast indulged, though they be the foulest which pollute mankind, yet if from thine heart thou hast learned to pray—

"Prayer is the breath of God in man,
Returning whence it came"—

thou canst not perish with God's breath in thee.

On a tradesman's table I noticed a book labelled WANT BOOK. What a practical suggestion for a man of prayer! He should put down all his needs on the tablets of his heart, and then present his *want book* to his God. If we knew all our need, what a large want book we should require! How comforting to know that Jesus has a supply book, which exactly meets our want book! Promises, providences, and divine visitations, combine to meet the necessities of all the faithful.

Prayer pulls the rope below and the great bell rings above in the ears of God. Some scarcely stir the bell, for they pray so languidly; others give but an occasional pluck at the rope; but he who wins with heaven is the man who grasps the rope boldly and pulls continuously, with all his might.

43. Procrastination

A number of men are upstairs in a house, amusing themselves with a game of cards. What is that? The window is red! What is that cry in the streets? *"The house is on fire!"* says one.

"Oh," answers another; "shuffle the cards again, let us finish the game; we have plenty of time."

"Fire! Fire! Fire!" The cry rises more sharply from the streets, but the gamblers continue their game. One of them swaggeringly boasts, "It's all right, my brave boys, yon door leads to the roof, and we can get out at the last minute. I know the way over the leads—it's all right, go ahead with the game."

Presently one of them nervously inquires: "Are you sure that we can get through that door?" And he goes to try, but finds it locked.

"Never mind," is the answer, "I have the key."

"But are you sure you have the key?"

"Oh, yes! I am sure I have; here it is; try it for yourself, and do not be such a coward, man; try it."

The man tries the key. "It will not turn," says he.

"Let me try," says his friend. He puts it in the lock, but, lo! it will not turn! *"O, God!"* he shrieks, *"it's the wrong key!"*

Now, sirs, will ye go back to your game again? No; now they will strain every nerve, and labour with might and main to open the door, only to find that it is all too late for them to escape.

So many of our hearers are saying: "Oh, yes! what the preacher says is well enough, but you know we can repent whenever we like. We have power to obtain the grace of God whenever we please. We know the way. Have we not been told over and over again simply to trust Christ?—and we can do that whenever we please—we are safe enough." *Ah, but suppose you cannot believe whenever you please?* Suppose the day shall come when you shall call upon the Lord, and He will not answer; when you shall stretch out your hand, but no man shall regard? Suppose you should one day cry, "Lord, Lord, open to us," and the answer should be, "I never knew you, depart, ye cursed"?

O, procrastinator, if you think that you can repent now, *why do you not repent now?* You believe that you have full power to do so. Oh, do it, do it, and do not trifle with that power, lest when the power is gone, you find, too late, that in one sense you never possessed it!

44. Promises Countersigned by Faith

Some bank bills require the signature of the person for whom they are drawn, and they would not be payable at the bank, though regularly signed, unless countersigned by the person to whom they are due. Many of the Lord's promises are drawn in like fashion. Armed with such promises, you go to the bank of prayer, and you ask to have them fulfilled; but your petitions are not granted because they need to be countersigned by the sign-manual of your faith in them; and when God has given you grace to believe His promise, then shall you see the fulfilment of it with your eyes.

Give me ten thousand pounds, and one reverse of fortune may scatter it all away; but let me have a spiritual hold of this divine assurance—*"The Lord is my shepherd, I shall not want"* —then I am all right—I am set up for life. I cannot break with such stock as this in hand. I never can be a bankrupt, for I hold this security— *"The Lord is my shepherd, I shall not want."* Do not give me ready money now; give a check-book, and let me draw what I like. This is what God does with the believer. He does not immediately transfer his inheritance to him, but lets him draw what he needs out of the riches of His fulness in Christ Jesus.

45. THE DIGNITY OF CHRISTIAN SERVICE

It seems to me that every Sunday-school teacher who discharges his trust is certainly a "Right Honourable." He teaches his congregation and preaches to his class. A minister may preach to more, and he to less, but still he is doing the same work, though in a smaller sphere. I can sympathize with Mr. Carey, when he said of his son Felix, who left the missionary work to become an ambassador: "Felix has drivelled into an ambassador"; meaning to say that he was once a great person as a missionary, but he had accepted a comparatively insignificant office.

So, I think, we may say of the Sabbath-school teacher who gives up his work because he cannot attend to it, that he drivels into a merchant. If he forsakes his teaching because he finds there is so much else to do, he drivels into something less than he was before—with one exception, if he is obliged to give up in order to attend to his own family, and makes that family his Sabbath-school class, there is no drivelling there. He stands in the same position as before.

46. Courage Necessary

You tell me a deacon has thrown cold water upon your efforts. Cold water! Does that discourage you? Are you in a fluster about that? What would you have done if, like old Latimer, you had been called to take off your garments some cold morning in Smithfield, to be warmed after an awful fashion, by standing on a stake to play the man and light up a candle for your God? The pity that some people sigh for on account of their petty persecutions and troubles, it is a shame to ask and a waste to give. Cannot we suffer for Christ? If we cannot, it must be because our spiritual strength must be low, and our life unhealthy. O, for more love, and more faith, and more spiritual vigour in our constitutions, and then we shall clear half our difficulties at a running leap, and scarcely call them other than light afflictions which are but for a moment, and are not worthy to be compared with the glory which shall be revealed in us.

47. Do Something

There is not a spider hanging on the king's wall but hath its errand; there is not a nettle that groweth in the corner of the churchyard but hath its purpose; there is not a single insect fluttering in the breeze but accomplisheth some divine decree; and I will never have it that God created any man, especially any Christian man, to be a blank, and to be a nothing. He made you for an end. Find out what that end is; find out your niche and fill it. If it be ever so little, if it is only to be a hewer of wood and drawer of water, do something in this great battle for God and truth.

48. Strength for Service

In the battle of Salamanca, when Wellington bade one of his officers advance with his troops and occupy a gap which the duke perceived in the lines of the French, the general rode up to him, and said: "My lord, I will do the work, but first give me a grasp of that conquering right hand of yours." He received a hearty grip, and away he rode to the deadly encounter.

Often has my soul said to her Captain: "My Lord, I will do that work if Thou wilt give me a grip of Thy conquering hand." Oh, what power it puts into a man when he gets a grip of Christ, and Christ gets a grip of him! Fellowship with Christ is the fountain of the church's strength.

49. Personal Work

I once heard a story of an American who declared he could fight the whole British army, and when he was asked how he could draw so long a bow as that, he said: "Why, this is what I would do. I know I am the best swordsman in the world, so I would go and challenge one Britisher, and kill him; then take another, and kill him. Thus," said he, "I only want time enough and I would kill the whole British army."

It was a ridiculous boast, but there is something in it which I could not bring out so well in any other way. If we want to conquer the world for the Lord Jesus Christ, rest assured we must do it in the Yankee's fashion; we must take men one by one, and these ones must be brought to Christ, or otherwise the great mass must remain untouched. Do not imagine for a moment that you are going to convert a nation at once. You are to convert the men of that nation one by one, through the power of God's Holy Spirit. It is not for you to suit your machinery, and arrange your plans, for the moving of a mass as such; you must look to the salvation of the units.

50. Unfaithful Service

What a dreadful thing it must be to be an unfaithful preacher on a dying bed! To be upon one's bed when life is over; to have had great opportunities, mighty congregations, and to have been so diligent about something else as to have neglected to preach the full and free gospel of our Lord Jesus Christ!

Methinks as I laid in my bed a-dying, I could see spectres and grim things in the room. One would come and stare upon me and say: "Ah! you are dying. Remember how many times I sat in the front of the gallery and listened to you, but you never once told me to escape from the wrath to come. You talked about something I did not understand, but the simple matter of the gospel you never preached to me, and I died in doubt and trembling. And now you are coming to me to the hell which I have inherited because you were unfaithful." And when in our grey and dying age we see the generations which have grown up around our pulpits, we shall think of them all. We shall think of the time when as striplings we first began to preach. We shall recollect the youths that then crowded, then the men, and the grey heads that passed away. And methinks as they come on in grim procession, they will every one leave a fresh curse upon our conscience because we were unfaithful.

The death-bed of a man who has murdered his fellows, of some grim tyrant who has let the bloodhounds of war loose upon mankind, must be an awful thing. When the soldier, and the soldier's widow, and the murdered man of peace rise up before him; when the smoke of devastated countries seems to blow into his eyes and make them sore and red; when the blood of men hangs on his conscience like a great red pall; when bloody murder, the grim chamberlain, draws red curtains round his bed, and when he begins to approach the last end where the murderer must inherit his dreary doom, it must be a fearful time indeed. But methinks to have murdered souls must be more awful still—to have distributed poison to children instead of bread, to have given them stones when they asked us for right food, to have taught them error when we ought to have taught them the truth as it is in Jesus, or to have spoken to them with cold listlessness when earnestness was needed.

John Brown, of Haddington, said to a young minister, who complained of the smallness of his congregation, "It is as large a one as you will want to give account for in the day of judgment." The admonition is appropriate; not to ministers alone, but to all teachers.

51. The Song of Heaven and Earth

Heaven singeth evermore. Before the throne of God, angels and redeemed saints extol His name. And this world is singing, too: sometimes with the loud noise of the rolling thunder, of the boiling sea, of the dashing cataract, of the lowing cattle; often with that still, solemn harmony which floweth from the vast creation when in its silence it praiseth God.

Such is the song which gushes in silence from the mountain lifting its head to the sky, covering its face sometimes with the wings of mist, and at other times unveiling its snow-white brow before its Maker, and reflecting back His sunshine, gratefully thanking Him for the light with which it has been made to glisten, and for the gladness of which it is the solitary spectator, as in its grandeur it looks down upon the laughing valleys.

The tune to which heaven and earth are set is the same. In heaven they sing, *"The Lord be exalted: let His name be magnified forever."* And the earth singeth the same: *"Great art Thou in Thy works, O Lord! and unto Thee be glory."*

52. Salvation by Grace

Salvation is altogether of grace, grace which comes from God in His mercy to man in his helplessness.

The gospel does not come to you asking something of you, but its hands are laden with gifts more precious than gold, which it freely bestows upon guilty men. It comes to us, not as a reward for the obedient and deserving, but as a merciful boon for the disobedient and undeserving. It treats with us, not upon the ground of justice, but upon terms of pure mercy. It asks no price and exacts no purchase. It comes as a benefactor, not as a judge. In the gospel God giveth liberally and upbraideth not.

We are accustomed not only to say "grace," but "free grace." It has been remarked that this is a tautology. So it is, but it is a blessed one, for it makes the meaning doubly clear and leaves no room for mistake. Since it is evidently objectionable to those who dislike the doctrine intended, it is manifestly forcible, and therefore we will keep to it. We feel no compunction in ringing such a silver bell twice over—grace, free grace. Lest any should imagine that grace can be otherwise than free, we shall continue to say, not only grace, but free grace, so long as we preach.

Only give intimation that goods are to be had *gratis*, and your store will be besieged by customers. Those who want us to notice their wares are often crafty enough to put at the head of their advertisement what is not true: *"To be given away"*; but salvation's grand advertisement is true. Salvation is everything for nothing—pardon free, Christ free, heaven free. *"Come, buy wine and milk without money and without price."*

53. SALVATION BY WORKS

The doctrine of salvation by works would silence the hallelujahs of heaven. Hush, ye choristers, what meaning is there in your song? You are chanting, *"Unto Him that loved us, and washed us front our sins in His own blood."* But why sing ye so? If salvation be by works, your ascriptions of praise are empty flatteries. You ought to sing, "Unto ourselves who kept our garments clean, to us be glory forever and ever"; or at least, "Unto ourselves whose acts made the Redeemer's work effectual be a full share of praise." But a self-lauding note was never heard in heaven, and therefore we feel sure that the doctrine of self-justification is not of God. I charge you, renounce it as the foe of God and man.

Be it known unto you that God's grace will never share the work with man's merit. As oil will not combine with water, so neither will heavenly mercy and human merit mix together. The apostle says: *"If by grace, then it is no more of works; otherwise, grace is no more grace. But if it be of works, then it is no more grace: otherwise work is no more work."* You must either have salvation wholly because you deserve it, or wholly because God graciously bestows it although you do not deserve it. You receive it at the Lord's hands either as a debt or as a charity—there can be no mingling of the ideas.

I grow warm upon such a subject as this, for my indignation rises against that which does dishonour to my Lord, and frustrates His grace. This is a sin so gross that even the heathen cannot commit it. They have never heard of the grace of God, and therefore they cannot put a slight upon it. When they perish, it will be with a far lighter doom than those who have been told that God is gracious and ready to pardon, and yet turn on their heel and wickedly boast of innocence, and pretend to be clean in the sight of God. This is a sin which devils cannot commit. With all the obstinacy of their rebellion, they can never reach to this. They have never had the sweet notes of free grace and dying love ringing in their ears, and therefore they have never refused the heavenly invitation. What has never been presented to their acceptance cannot be the object of their rejection. Thus, then, my reader, if you should fall into this deep ditch you will sink lower than the heathen, lower than Sodom and Gomorrah, and lower than the devil himself

54. Subtlety of Satan

Satan never brushes the feathers of his birds the wrong way. He generally deals with them according to their tastes and likings. He flavours his bait to his fish.

55. SELF-RIGHTEOUSNESS

Self-righteousness is *natural to our fallen humanity*. Hence it is the essence of all false religions. Be they what they may, they all agree in seeking salvation by man's own deeds. He who worships his idols will torture his body, will fast, will perform long pilgrimages, and do or endure anything in order to merit salvation. Go where you may, the natural religion of fallen man is salvation by his own merits. An old divine has well said, every man is born a heretic upon this point, and he naturally gravitates towards this heresy in one form or another. Self-salvation, either by his personal worthiness, or by his repentance, or by his resolves, is a hope ingrained in human nature, and very hard to remove. This foolishness is bound up in the heart of every child, and who shall get it out of him?

This erroneous idea arises partly from *ignorance*, for men are ignorant of the law of God, and of what holiness really is. If they knew that even an evil thought is a breach of the law, and that the law once broken in any point is altogether violated, they would be at once convinced that there can be no righteousness by the law to those who have already offended against it. They are also in great ignorance concerning themselves, for those very persons who talk about self-righteousness are, as a rule, openly chargeable with fault; and if not, were they to sit down and really look at their own lives, they would soon perceive even in their best works such impurity of motive beforehand, or such pride and self-congratulation afterwards, that they would see the gloss taken off from all their performances, and they would be utterly ashamed of them.

Nor is it ignorance alone which leads men to self-righteousness; they are also deceived by *pride*. Man cannot endure to be saved on the footing of mercy. He loves not to plead guilty and throw himself on the favour of the great King; he cannot brook to be treated as a pauper, and blessed as a matter of charity; he desires to have a finger in his own salvation, and claim at least a little credit for it. Proud man will not have heaven itself upon terms of grace, but so long as he can he sets up one plea or another, and holds to his own righteousness as though it were his life.

This self-confidence also rises from wicked *unbelief* for through his self-conceit man will not believe God. Nothing is more plainly revealed in Scripture than this—that by the works of the law shall no man be justified. Yet men in some shape or other stick to the hope of legal righteousness; they will have it that they must prepare for grace, or assist mercy, or in some degree deserve eternal life. They prefer their own flattering prejudices to the declaration of the heart-searching God. The testimony of the Holy Spirit concerning the deceitfulness of the heart is cast aside, and the declaration of God that there is none that doeth good, no, not one, is altogether denied. Is not this a great evil?

Self-righteousness is also much promoted by the almost universal *spirit of trifling* which is now abroad. Only while men trifle with themselves can they entertain the idea of personal merit before God. He who comes to serious thought, and begins to understand the character of God, abhors himself in dust and ashes, and is forever silenced as to any thought of self-justification. It is because we do not seriously examine our condition that we think ourselves rich and increased in goods. A man may fancy that he is prospering in business, and yet he may be going back in the world. If he does not face his books, or take stock, he may be living in a fool's paradise, spending largely when on the verge of bankruptcy. Many think well of themselves because they never think seriously. They do not look below the surface, and hence they are deceived by appearances. The most troublesome business to many men is thought; and the last thing they will do is to weigh their actions, or test their motives, or ponder their ways, to see whether things be right with them. Self-righteousness being supported by ignorance, by pride, by unbelief, and the natural superficiality of the human mind, is strongly entrenched, and cannot readily be driven out of men.

Yet self-righteousness is *evidently evil*, for it makes light of sin. It talks of merit in the case of one who has already transgressed, and boasts of excellence in reference to a fallen and depraved creature. It prattles of little faults, small failures, and slight omissions, and so makes sin to be a venial error which may be readily overlooked. Not so faith in God; for though it recognizes pardon, yet that pardon is seen to come in a way which proves sin to be exceeding sinful. On the other hand, the doctrine of salvation by works has not a word of comfort in it for the fallen. It gives to the elder son all that his proud heart can claim, but for the prodigal it has no welcome. The law has no invitation for the sinner, for it knows nothing of mercy. If salvation be by the works of the law, what must become of the guilty, and the fallen, and the abandoned? By what hopes can these be recalled? This unmerciful doctrine bars the door of hope, and hands over the lost ones to the executioner, in order that the proud Pharisee may air his boastful righteousness, and thank God that he is not as other men are.

It is the intense selfishness of this doctrine which condemns it as an evil thing. It naturally exalts self. If a man conceives that he will be saved by his own works he thinks himself somewhat, and glorifies in the dignity of human nature: when he has been attentive to religious exercises he rubs his hands and feels he deserves well of his Maker; he goes home to repeat his prayers, and ere he falls asleep he wonders how he can have grown to be so good and so superior to those around him. All the while, he considers himself to be very humble, and is often amazed at his own condescension. What is this but a hateful spirit? God, who sees the heart, loathes it.

56. The Common Prison

I dreamt I came to a common prison, where innumerable souls are shut up. It were useless to attempt to count them; they are legion; their number is ten thousand times ten thousand. It is *the ward of sin*. All the human race have been prisoners here, and those who this day are perfectly at liberty, once wore the heavy chain, and were immured within the black walls of this enormous prison.

I stepped into it, and to my surprise, instead of hearing (as I had expected) notes of mourning and lament, I heard loud and repeated bursts of laughter. The mirth was boisterous and obstreperous. The profane were cursing and blaspheming; others were shouting as though they had found great spoil. I looked into the faces of some of the criminals, and saw sparkling gaiety: their aspect was rather that of wedding-guests than prisoners. Walking to and fro, I noticed captives who boasted that they were free, and when I spoke to them of their prison-house, and urged them to escape, they resented my advice, saying, "We were born free, and were never in bondage unto any man." They bade me prove my words; and when I pointed to the irons on their wrists, they laughed at me, and said that these were ornaments which gave forth music as they moved; it was only my dull and sombre mind, they said, which made me talk of clanking fetters and jingling chains. There were men fettered hard and fast to foul and evil vices, and these called themselves free-livers, while others whose very thoughts were bound, for the iron had entered into their soul, with braggart looks cried out to me that they were free-thinkers.

Truly, I had never seen such bond-slaves in my life before, nor any so fast manacled as these; but ever did I mark as I walked this prison through and through that the most fettered thought themselves the most free, and those who were in the darkest part of the dungeon thought they had most light, and those whom I considered to be the most wretched, and the most to be pitied, were the very ones who laughed the most, and raved most madly and boisterously in their mirth. I looked with sorrow, but as I looked, I saw a bright spirit touch a prisoner on the shoulder, who thereon withdrew with the shining one. He went out, and I knew (for I had read the text—*"The Lord looseth the prisoners"*) that the prisoner had been loosened from the house of bondage. But I noted that as he went forth his late bond-fellows laughed and pointed with the finger, and called him sniveller, hypocrite, mean pretender, and all ill names, until the prison walls rang and rang again with their mirthful contempt.

I watched, and saw the mysterious visitant touch another, and then another, and another, and they disappeared. The common conversation of the prison said that they had gone mad, that they were become slaves, or miserable fanatics, whereas I knew that they were gone to be free forever, emancipated from every bond.

What struck me most was, that the prisoners who were touched with the finger of delivering love were frequently the worst of the whole crew. I marked one who had blasphemed, but the Divine hand touched him, and he went weeping out of the gate. I saw another who had often scoffed the loudest when he had seen others led away, but he went out as quietly as a lamb. I observed some, whom I thought to be the least depraved of them all, but they were left, and oftentimes the blackest sinners of the whole company were first taken, and I remembered that I had somewhere in an old book read these words— *"The publicans and the harlots enter into the kingdom of God before you."*

As I gazed intently, I saw some of these men who had once been prisoners come back again into the prison—not in the same dress which they had worn before, but arrayed in white robes, looking like new creatures. They began to talk with their fellow-prisoners; and, oh! how sweetly did they speak! They told them there was liberty to be had, that yonder door would open, and that they might escape. They pleaded with their fellow-men, even unto tears. I saw them sit down and talk with them till they wept upon their necks, urging them to escape, pleading as though it were their own life that was at stake. At first I hoped within myself that all the company of prisoners would rise and cry, "Let us be free." But no; the more these men pleaded the harder the others seemed to grow—and, indeed, I found it so when I sought myself to be an ambassador to these slaves of sin. Wherever the finger of the shining one was felt, our pleadings easily prevailed; but save and except in those who were thus touched by the heavenly messenger, all our exhortations fell upon deaf ears, and we left that den of iniquity crying, *"Who hath believed our report, and to whom is the arm of the Lord revealed?"*

Then I was cast into a muse, as I considered what a marvel of mercy it was that I myself should be free; for well do I remember when I spurned every invitation of love, when I hugged my chains, dreamed my prison garb to be a royal robe, and took the meals of the prison, called the pleasures of sin, and relished them as sweet, yea, dainty morsels, fit for princes.

57. BITTEN BY A SERPENT

What an awful thing it is to be bitten by a serpent! I daresay some of you recollect the case of Gurling, one of the keepers of the reptiles in the Zoological Gardens. It happened in October, 1852.

This unhappy man was about to part with a friend who was going to Australia, and, according to the wont of many, he must needs drink with him. He drank considerable quantities of gin, and though he would probably have been in a great passion if anyone had called him drunk, yet reason and common-sense had evidently become overpowered. He went back to his post at the gardens in an excited state. He had some months before seen an exhibition of snake-charming, and this was on his poor, muddled brain. He must emulate the Egyptians, and play with serpents. First he took out of its cage a Morocco venom-snake, put it round his neck, twisted it about, and whirled it round about him. Happily for him, it did not arouse itself so as to bite.

The assistant-keeper cried out, "For God's sake, put back the snake!" But the foolish man replied, "I am inspired."

Putting back the venom-snake, he exclaimed, "Now for the cobra." This deadly serpent was somewhat torpid with the cold of the previous night, and therefore the rash man placed it in his bosom till it revived and glided downwards till its head appeared below the back of his waistcoat. He took it by the body, about a foot from the head, and then seized it lower down by the other hand, intending to hold it by the tail and swing it round his head. He held it for an instant opposite to his face, and, like a flash of lightning, the serpent struck him between the eyes. The blood streamed down his face, and he called for help, but his companion fled in horror, and, as he told the jury, he did not know how long he was gone, for he was "in a maze."

When assistance arrived, Gurling was sitting on a chair, having restored the cobra to its place. He said, "I am a dead man." They put him in a cab, and took him to the hospital. First his speech went, he could only point to his poor throat and moan; then his vision failed him, and lastly his hearing. His pulse gradually sank, and in one hour from the time at which he had been struck he was a corpse. There was only a little mark upon the bridge of his nose, but the poison spread over the body, and he was a dead man.

I tell you that story that you may use it as a parable and learn *never to play with sin*, and also in order to bring vividly before you what it is to be bitten by a serpent.

Suppose that Gurling could have been cured by looking at a piece of brass, would it not have been good news for him? There was no remedy for that poor infatuated creature, but there is a remedy for you. For men who have been bitten by the fiery serpent of sin, Jesus Christ is lifted up: not for you only who are as yet playing with the serpent, not for you only who have warmed it in your bosom, and felt it creeping over your flesh, but for you who are actually bitten, and are mortally wounded. If any man be bitten so that he has become diseased with sin, and feels the deadly venom in his blood, it is for him that Jesus is set forth today. *"As Moses lifted up the serpent in the wilderness, even so must the Son of man be lifted up: that whosoever believeth in Him should not perish, but have eternal life."*

58. THE SINNER'S BEST PLEA

A man called at my house some time ago for charity; an arrant beggar, I have no doubt. Thinking that the man's rags and poverty were real, I gave him a little money, some of my clothes, and a pair of shoes.

After he had put them on and gone out, I thought, "Well, after all, I have done you a bad turn very likely, for you will not get so much money now as before, because you will not look so wretched an object."

Happening to go out a quarter of an hour afterwards, I saw my friend, but he was not wearing the clothes I had given him, not he; why, I should have ruined his business if I could have compelled him to look respectable. He had been wise enough to slip down an archway, take all the good clothes off, and put his rags on again. Did I blame him? Yes, for being a rogue, but not for carrying on his business in a business-like manner. He only wore his proper livery, for rags are the livery of a beggar. The more ragged he looked, the more he would get.

Just so it is with you. If you are to go to Christ, do not put on your good doings and feelings, or you will get nothing; go in your sins, they are your livery. Your ruin is your argument for mercy;

your poverty is your plea for heavenly alms; and your need is the motive for heavenly goodness.

59. Temptation

When a traveller was asked whether he did not admire the admirable structure of some stately building, "No," he said, "for I've been at Rome, where better are to be seen every day."

O believer, if the world tempt thee with its rare sights and curious prospects, thou mayest well scorn them, having been, by contemplation, in heaven, and being able, by faith, to see infinitely better delights every hour of the day. *"This is the victory that overcometh the world, even our faith."*

60. Free Thought

There is a notion abroad that thought is free; but I remember reading that although thoughts are toll-free, they are not hell-free; and that saying quite agrees with the good old Book. We cannot be summoned before an earthly court for thinking; but, depend upon it, we shall have to be tried for it at the Last Assizes.[2] Evil thoughts are the marrow of sin; the malt that sin is brewed from; the tinder which catches the sparks of the devil's temptations; the churn in which the milk of imagination is churned into purpose and plan; the nest in which all evil birds lay their eggs. Be certain, then, that as sure as fire burns brushwood as well as logs, God will punish thoughts of sin as well as deeds of sin.

---

[2] That is "Last Judgment."

www.ingramcontent.com/pod-product-compliance
Lightning Source LLC
Chambersburg PA
CBHW011131070526
44583CB00023B/2987